To:

From:

ROCK SOLID
LEADERSHIP

How Great Leaders Exceed Expectations

ROBIN CROW

My thanks to
David and Marc Muench
whose photos are featured in this book.

Pages: 1, 8, 20, 26-27, 28, 48-49, 50-51, 56, 60-61, 66,
70, 74-75, 86, 96, 104, 108-109, 112-113.

Design: Vieceli Design Company, West Dundee, Illinois

Published by Simple Truths, an imprint of Sourcebooks, Inc.
P.O. Box 4410, Naperville, Illinois 60567-4410
(630) 961-3900
Fax: (630) 961-2168
www.sourcebooks.com

Printed and bound in China.
FCP 10 9 8 7 6 5 4 3 2

Table of Contents

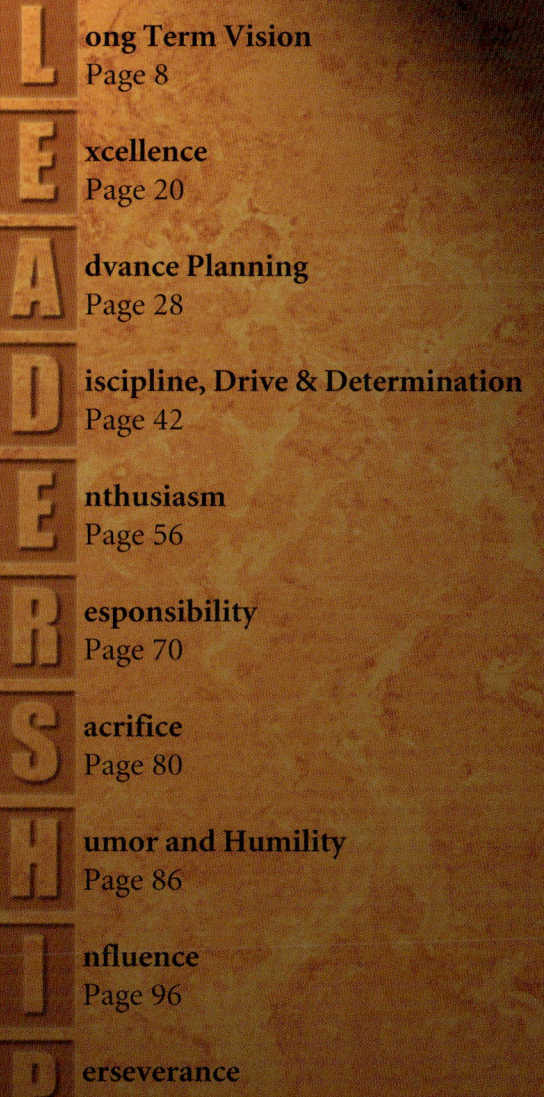

Who's in CHARGE?

At last… our family vacation — but looking out the window from my airline seat, all I could see were threatening clouds in every direction. The rain had been constant all morning and now the pilot was putting the pedal to the metal and there we were, me and my family, streaking down the rain-soaked runway rocketing into those thunder clouds like a tin can shot out of a cannon ascending thousands of feet every minute. It's always such a helpless feeling, hurdling through the air at 500 miles an hour, then we hit one of those air pockets and bam, the plane drops. I quickly look over at the flight attendant to see if they look concerned. Whew… they seem fine, so there I sit looking like everything's cool, but in reality I'm rethinking the whole idea of getting on board in the first place. OK, maybe I'm being a bit overdramatic, but the whole idea of flying can be disconcerting sometimes, to say the least. On the other hand, I've taken off in weather just like this countless times before and lived to fly another day, so it shouldn't be a big deal. After all, whoever's in charge knows what they're doing. Right?

We had only been airborne for two or three minutes when there was a blinding flash and a shotgun-like explosion. The whole plane shook! Had a bomb gone off? Had someone just fired a gun? Did we blow out an engine? NOT NOW, I'M ON VACATION!! I think I speak for everyone on board when I say it was unnerving and with all the terrorist activities going on in the world, the tension was so thick you could cut it with a knife. It seemed like an eternity as we all sat there in silence, then at last, the captain's voice — "Well, that will get your heart pumping," making light of that gut wrenching feeling we all had in the pits of our stomachs. "We've just been struck by lightning," like it was no big deal. Lightning?! That can't be good. Can it?

My career requires that I fly constantly, yet I've never experienced being in a plane that was struck by lightning. Shouldn't we turn around and land?

Mr. Pilot… please tell us the plane's made for this kind of thing — that it happens all the time. I began asking myself…Who's in charge? One thing was for sure, I'm trusting my life to a couple of pilots who I don't know anything about. How about their leadership ability? How mentally and emotionally equipped are they to handle extreme adversity? Maybe they should pass out résumés stating how many air miles they've logged and perhaps their college grade point average. After all… my children's lives are in their hands. Think about it… what if that pilot's just had an argument with his wife? What if he's not feeling good? What if he's had too much coffee?

Why would I even consider putting my life in someone's hands like this? Why would I put my children's lives in the hands of people I've never met? **The reason starts and ends with Leadership.** We wouldn't consciously think of the pilot, flight attendant or airline mechanic as leaders in the traditional sense. But over time, we have developed a trust in the leadership it collectively takes to create safe air travel day in and day out. As if building jet airplanes wasn't impressive enough… through leadership and teamwork, all the systems of safety, timing, scheduling and other mind-boggling logistics are organized to get us safely from one place to another. In the back of my mind I usually rest easy knowing that someone has put together an extraordinary master plan that proves to be safe and reliable.

Leadership is about taking charge and influencing others to follow your vision. It's about going against the odds and accepting responsibility for the outcomes along the way. It's about exceeding expectations by going the extra mile, by consistently going the distance to insure success.

The principles of leadership I'll share in this book are hard-learned lessons that I've experienced on my journey from struggling musician to national recording artist, then on to entrepreneur and business owner. I've had my share of successes, but for every success, I have failed many times. But from each one of those failures I've discovered that becoming successful in life comes down to applying a few very simple, but important principles of **LEADERSHIP**. So let's get started.

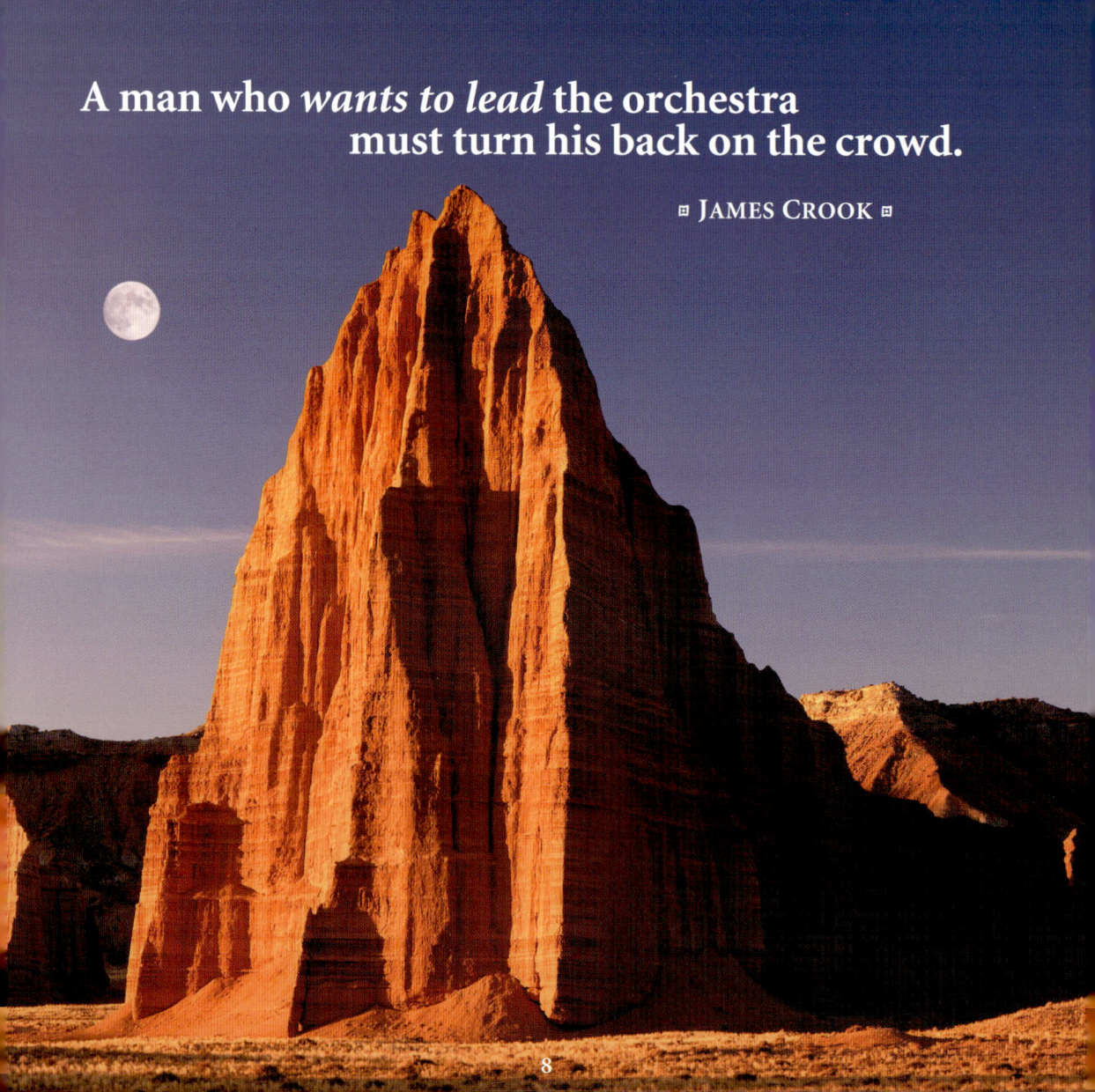

A man who *wants to lead* the orchestra
must turn his back on the crowd.

▫ JAMES CROOK ▫

LONG TERM VISION

One of my favorite quotes is: "A leader's job is to look into the future and see the company, not as it is, but as it should be." In *The Essence of Leadership*, Mac Anderson wrote about Howard Schultz, the founder of Starbucks and how he turned his vision into reality.

Early on, Schultz realized that the key to his success was to recruit well-educated people who were eager to communicate their passion for coffee. This, he felt, would be his competitive

True leadership must be for the *benefit* of the followers, not the *enrichment* of the leaders.

▫ **ROBERT TOWNSEND** ▫

advantage in an industry where turnover was 300 percent a year. To hire the best people, he also knew he must be willing to pay them more than the going wage and offer health benefits that weren't available elsewhere. He saw that part-time people made up two-thirds of his employee base and no one in the restaurant industry offered benefits to part-timers. Schultz went to work in an effort to sell his board of directors to increase expenses while most restaurant executives in the 1980's were looking for ways to cut costs. Initially Schultz's pleas to investors and the board fell on deaf ears because Starbucks was still losing money. But Schultz was persistent. He was looking long term and was committed to growing the business with passionate people. He won and he said many times afterward that this decision was one of the most important decisions, if not the most important, that he had made at Starbucks. His employee retention rate was about five times the industry average, but more importantly, he could attract people with great attitudes who made their customers feel welcome and at home.

As a leader, Schultz realized early on that Starbucks wasn't a coffee business serving people… they were a people business serving coffee. This simple but powerful insight was the foundation on which his long term vision was built.

Those who can command themselves,

command others. ⬩ WILLIAM HAZLIFT ⬩

BRINGING YOUR VISION INTO FOCUS

To bring your vision into focus, imagine looking through a camera lens. That lens shows only the view in the direction you aim the camera. As you do this, everything else disappears. A leader knows the way to ignore the endless distractions is to stay focused. This also means staying focused on the positive, especially during times of adversity. Like Howard Schultz, a good leader knows the importance of holding on to that vision when times are tough. Leaders resist succumbing to fear, have faith and keep their eye fixed on where they're headed. They focus on solutions and possibilities. They focus on finding a way. That's how they follow through and exceed expectations.

When I was in the music business and in pursuit of a major record deal, my vision was strong but my focus was weak. People looked at me as a "man with a plan." Therefore I was able to get many others on board. For years I had a band, crew and manager, but I wasn't an effective leader. Why? I didn't understand that focus means not only zooming in on a pursuit, but in the process detaching

REAL LEADERS are *ordinary people* with extraordinary determinations.

◧ JOHN SEAMAN GARNS ◧

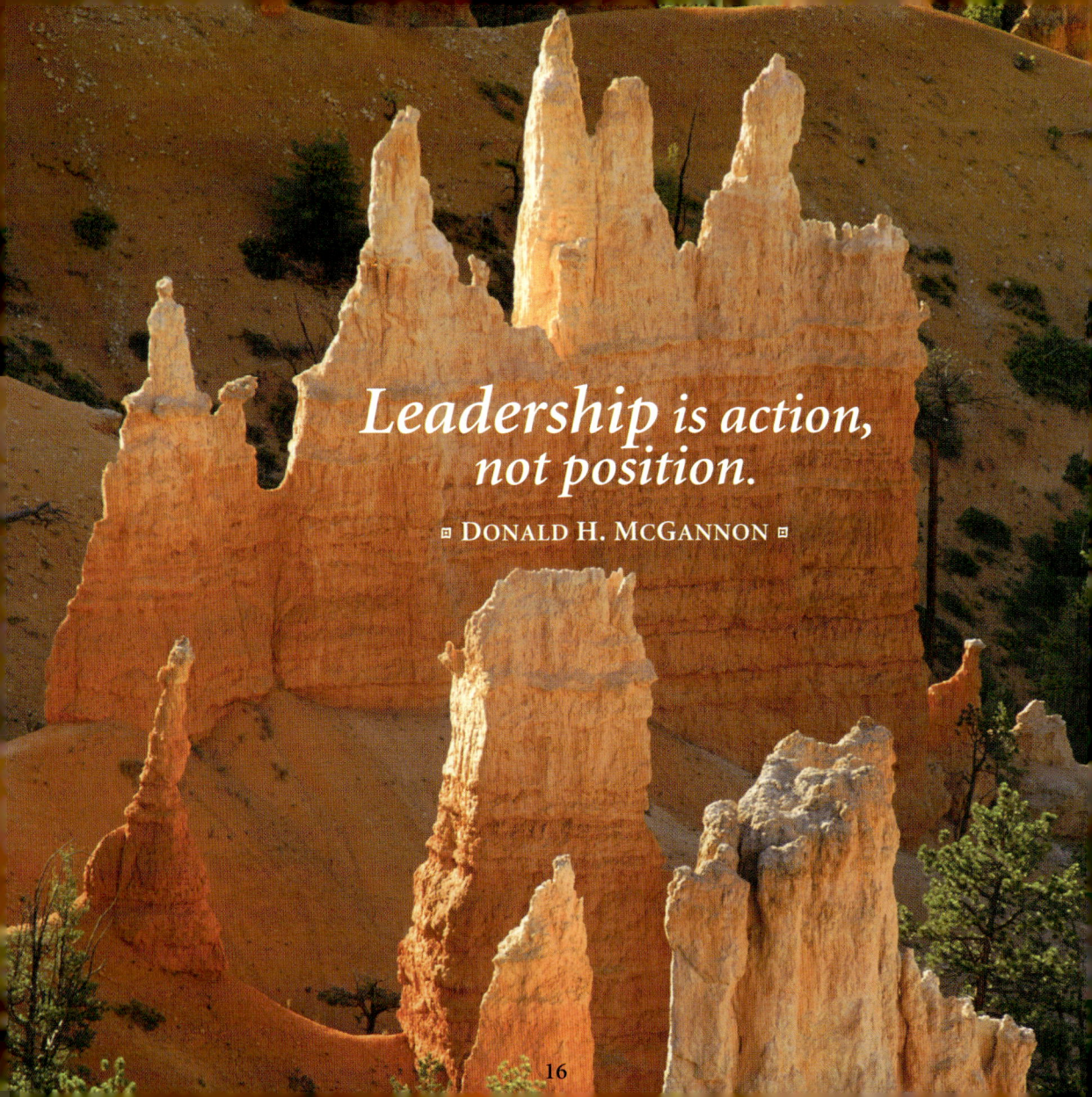

*Leadership is action,
not position.*

◻ Donald H. McGannon ◻

yourself from the other distractions that can drain your energy. My vision was to land a major record deal, but it wasn't until I was in my thirties that I finally admitted to myself that something had to change before I was going to get the results I was looking for. Once I did, I believe learning to focus made the difference in getting signed to RCA — even after receiving 132 rejection letters. That, in turn, provided me the opportunity to create my business, Dark Horse Recording, which then led to writing books and speaking professionally.

All of us have an inherent need for a clear sense of direction and purpose in life. We long to commit to something bigger and more important than ourselves. We want to feel like we are somehow making a contribution to the world. People are never really happy unless they are moving toward accomplishing something that is important to them. In other words, without a vision to latch on to, it's so easy to keep vacillating back and forth, making no progress, even in the smoothest of times. When you have a powerful, long-term vision for something, even against all odds and adversity, you will continue to make progress and people will want to get on board. Why? **Because everybody wants to be a part of something great.**

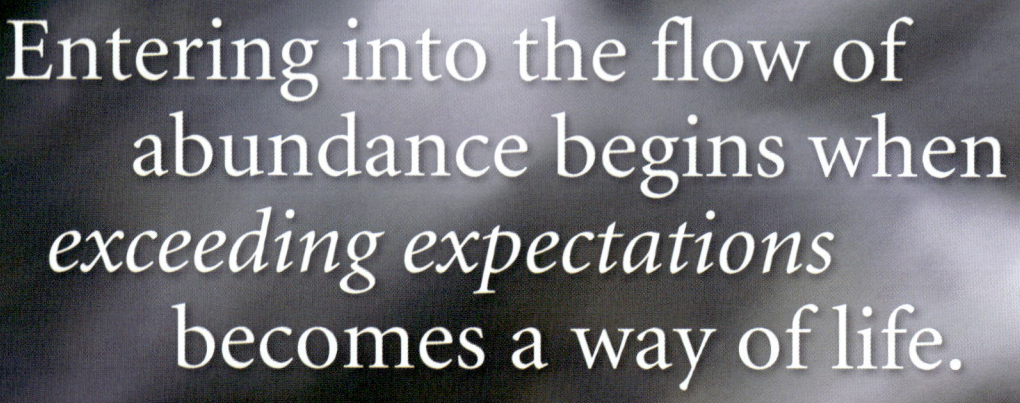

Entering into the flow of abundance begins when *exceeding expectations* becomes a way of life.

□ ROBIN CROW □

Nature… has proclaimed
that difficulty should
precede every work
of excellence.

◘ **QUINTILLIAN** ◘

EXCELLENCE

My friend Mike Rayburn once told me, "Robin, you have a great thing going. Famous people come to your home and pay you for it."

One of the first famous persons who came to Dark Horse Recording, which is my home and business, was Neil Diamond. It was July, 1997 when he came to Tennessee to record his next album, and I was thrilled he had chosen my studio. He brought his own

Strive for excellence, not

private chef who he flew in from L.A. He also flew in his own personal limo driver, two personal assistants and a recording engineer. And there he was, one of the biggest and most successful entertainers in the world… he had nothing to prove, yet he was always at the studio twelve hours a day, six days a week fine tuning each vocal performance, always challenging himself to a higher level of excellence. When he wasn't singing, he was in the lounge with his guitar going over each one of the songs he had written. Before Neil was done, he recorded 26 songs in their entirety… in order to be able

perfection. ▪ H. JACKSON BROWN, JR. ▪

to then select the absolute best for his album, which was titled *Tennessee Moon*. I have since witnessed hundreds of albums recorded at Dark Horse Recording, but I have never seen anyone aspire to achieve excellence to the level of Neil Diamond. Maybe that's why he's achieved such an extraordinary level of success. Year after year and decade after decade, he sells out his concerts and continues to produce platinum-selling records. This is a testament to what can happen when he consistently exceeds the expectations of his fans. When it comes to leadership, the greatest leaders are the ones who

Excellence is not an act, but a habit.

▣ **ARISTOTLE** ▣

continually work the hardest to improve… just like Neil Diamond. Remember, any time you want to step up your quality of life, any time you want to achieve an overwhelming goal, you've got to make a commitment to raise your standards. That's what striving for excellence is all about.

Sam Parker, in his book *212°… The Extra Degree*, cites a law of science that can change the way you think about Excellence. It did for me. At 211° water is hot… very hot. But, at 212° it boils and turns to steam; and steam can power a locomotive. Think about it. That one extra degree makes all the difference. And, usually it's that one extra degree of effort, in business and life, that separates the good from the great.

Ask yourself, "Have I ever had a great boss who didn't excel by going beyond what was expected of him/her? Have I ever had a great employee who didn't excel by going the extra mile? Let's even take it one step further. Have I ever known a great athlete, teacher or even parent who didn't embrace the 212° philosophy? They may not have known it, but they did. Parker warns that once you hear this simple, uncomplicated analogy about Excellence, it'll be hard to forget. Neil Diamond certainly embraced the 212° philosophy; and to me, it is a great definition of Excellence from which any leader can benefit.

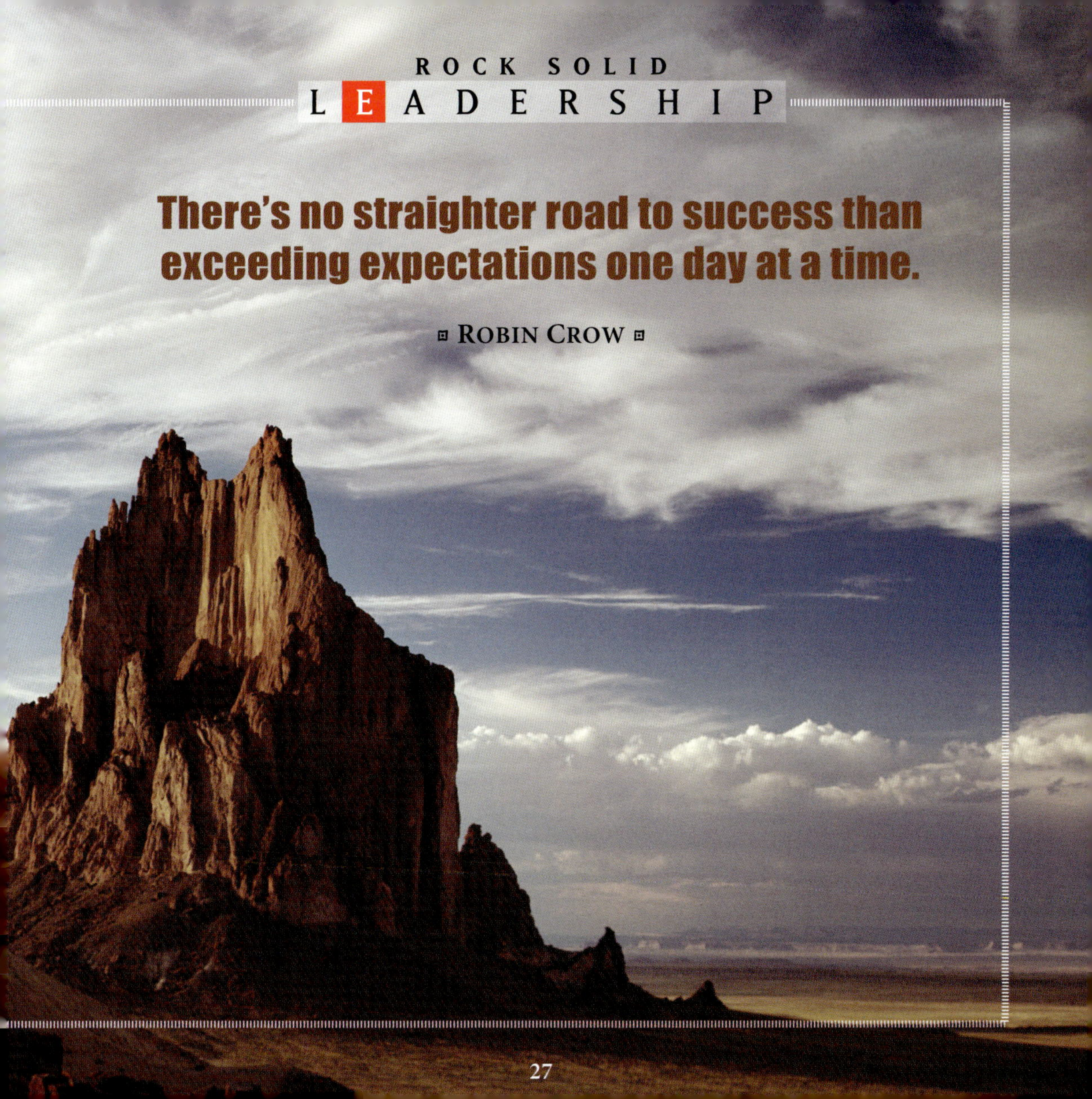

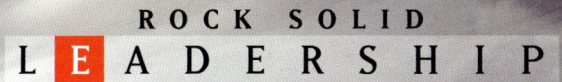

There's no straighter road to success than exceeding expectations one day at a time.

◻ ROBIN CROW ◻

The executive of the future will be rated by his *ability to anticipate* his problems rather than to *meet them as they come.*

◻ HOWARD COONLEY ◻

ADVANCE PLANNING

Advance planning is like taking the deep breath before the plunge. It's the calm before the storm. And that's when it's time to prepare, while it's calm, to ensure success no matter what unexpected storms might come up. Advance planning is the first step to exceeding expectations.

If exceeding expectations were an Olympic sport, my friend Phil Hickey would have a gold medal. In fact, if you've ever eaten at a Capitol Grill or a Long Horn Steak House, then you've probably had a taste of what Phil does to exceed expectations. He is the CEO and Chairman of Rare Hospitality, which owns and operates those restaurants all over the country. Thirteen years ago, when I first met Phil, I asked him about his business and he said "Robin, I've just given up a partnership in a small Tennessee restaurant chain and I recently bought this fledging restaurant… we've given it a complete face-lift and renamed it the Green Hills Grille. You should come

check it out some time." That's just what I did and from the moment
I stepped foot in that restaurant I knew it was destined to be an
absolute success. The entire staff, with their crisp cotton shirts and
colorful ties, reflected his enthusiasm and his passion for outstanding
customer service. Sometimes he would invite 50 or so of his friends
to the Green Hills Grille to eat, then he would pass out question-
naires asking for comments on service and food. There may be no
such thing as a free lunch, but this was a free dinner, and more
importantly it gave me an inside view of what he does to ensure
success. A year later Phil was opening his second restaurant in

Huntsville, Alabama, and he called me and said, "Robin, what do you say we take that Ryder truck you use for concerts, we'll fill it up with dishes, chairs and other supplies for opening night?" So there we were, driving to Huntsville and, as we pulled up to the intersection of the almost complete Green Hills Grille #2, he commented, "Robin, do you know that 14,000 north and southbound cars drive through that intersection every day, and the east and westbound traffic brings around 35,000 cars through each day?" It wasn't until the next day that it hit me… this guy is the DaVinci of advance planning. No wonder his Nashville restaurant is so successful… this gave me a glimpse at a leader who had carefully researched before taking action, who doesn't leave anything to chance. Thirteen years later he's

> The will to win is worthless if you do not
> have the will to prepare.
>
> ◪ **THANE YOST** ◪

Make your plans as fantastic as you like,
because *25 years* from now, they will seem mediocre.
Make your plans *ten times as great* as you first planned,
and *25 years* from now you will wonder why you
did not make them *50 times as great*.

◻ **HENRY CURTIS** ◻

gone from 2 to 302 restaurants and his company now has over 22,000 employees and earns over one billion dollars a year in sales. Phil will tell you that kind of success can only be achieved by exceeding the expectations of your customers on a daily basis.

Every leader knows how essential it is to survey the situation and detail their strategy. It sounds obvious… so why do so many people ignore this phase? I was one of them.

Last year, I created a photographic book called *The Power of an Idea.* It paints a visual story of some successes and failures I

*An intelligent plan is the first step
to success. The man who plans,
who knows where he is going, knows what
progress he is making and has a pretty good
idea where he will arrive. Planning is
the open road to your destination.
If you don't know where you are going,
how can you expect to get there?*

◻ BASIL S. WALSH ◻

encountered while attempting to become a successful recording artist and subsequent business owner. There's one section where I put in chronological order 25 postage stamp-sized pictures of my playing the guitar from the time I was 17 until 42. It's a stark reminder of how many years I spent spinning my wheels because I didn't have a focused plan. I didn't take the time to learn the truth about what it really takes to succeed in the music business. I didn't understand advance planning, I didn't ask questions, and I spent little or no time researching and creating a well thought through strategy. That was my story… I was always expending tons of energy vacillating back

"Success, in business as well as life, of people you surround

and forth but going nowhere. Instead of slowing down to gain perspective, develop a plan, then proceed ahead, I just practiced the philosophy of ready, fire, aim. But how can you expect to hit the target if you don't know what you're aiming for? All successful leaders have one thing in common — they know exactly what they want and they know where they're headed. All of us have the same 24 hours a day, or as I like to say, the same 8,760 hours in a year. (Or 8,784 hours in a leap year for those of you who give attention to detail.) What you do with that time will shape who you become as a leader.

is directly dependant on the quality yourself with." ⊡ PHIL HICKEY ⊡

EVERY MOVE YOU MAKE

If Sting was a motivational speaker he might say… "The very act of planning brings about clarity and focus to every breath you take and every move you make." Leaders who exceed expectations know the importance of being single-minded on the task at hand. A few important aspects of effective planning are to get focused on your outcome, prioritize, organize your time line and successfully delegate to maximize your efforts. We all do these steps almost unconsciously as we take on the simplest of tasks, like planning a party. But in order to successfully tackle something much larger, like meeting the goals and deadlines of your company, the more you plan in advance, the more successful your results will be. Bottom line… the more carefully you **plan**, the better prepared you'll be to make your **stand**.

DELEGATION

While you're engaged in all that advance planning, you'll need to decide who's going to carry out those actions. In the corporate world it's called OPE, which stands for "Other People's Efforts." There's no better way to leverage your energy than to enlist the efforts of others. Think of delegation as a way to greatly multiply your ability to get things done. To do this effectively there's a balance of managing and letting go. As you choose who you are going to put in charge of each task, take time to consider the strengths of each member of your team. This can be a critical factor for success. The more you surround yourself with people who have the skill sets and abilities that you need, the faster and more productive you can leverage your energy. Effective leaders know the more they can leverage their efforts, the more they can accomplish… a critical step to exceeding the expectations of their customers.

THE SHOW BEHIND THE SHOW

In the eighties and the early nineties I simply thought of it as "with a little help from my friends." Back then I toured college campuses endlessly, performing as many as one hundred concerts each year. There was an incredible amount of work that went into every show. Over the course of that time, I learned first hand the power of teamwork and delegation. Some days my crew and I would drive up to eight hundred miles just to get from one concert venue to the next. It was not uncommon to keep up this pace for five or six days, doing back-to-back shows, sleeping in shifts as we traveled in my converted Ryder truck with camper in the front and 6000 lbs. of gear in the rear. All of this required an enormous amount of planning and delegation. For each concert, we had to arrive seven hours before show time to get everything set up, so often there would be no time to stop by a hotel… it was straight to the venue, which was usually a college or university campus. There, we would be greeted by a dozen or so students who had volunteered to help us get things set up.

Each day, it was our job to quickly train those students to be an efficient stage crew, which meant assessing how we could put each person to work in a capacity that best suited them. It also meant taking the time to explain to our volunteers, step by step, how the next ten hours would play out. For every five minutes spent instructing and preparing each volunteer, they would in turn save us at least an hour of work… time well spent. I can't remember a more magical time, when, each day, we turned volunteers into a professional road crew.

No horse gets anywhere until he is harnessed.
No steam or gas ever drives anything until it is confined.
No Niagara is ever turned into light and power until
it is tunneled. No life ever grows great until it is
focused, dedicated, disciplined.

◻ HARRY EMERSON FOSDICK, D.D. ◻

DISCIPLINE, DRIVE & DETERMINATION

In the music industry, I've heard people say, "she's a natural," or "he's got so much talent." But what they didn't see are those musicians practicing five hours a day while their friends were outside playing football or at the movies. The real key to their success is self discipline. Scott Peck, in his book *The Road Less Traveled,* breaks discipline into four areas: delaying of gratification, acceptance of responsibility, dedication to the truth and balancing. He goes on to say that without discipline we can solve nothing. With some discipline we can solve some problems. And with total discipline we can solve all problems.

The price that must be paid for mastery is discipline. No one achieves lasting success without it. So from the moment you awake

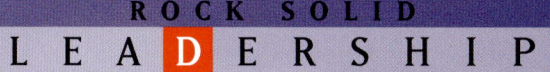

each day, devote yourself to the perfection of whatever you pursue. Do this and you will achieve self-mastery. Achieve self-mastery and you will have the makings of a great leader. Remember… a leader cannot take others further than he has gone himself. Discipline is all about cultivating powerful habits that become part of your lifestyle. At one point those habits can become your identity.

Consider this:

I am your constant companion.

      I am your greatest asset or heaviest burden.

I will push you up to success or down to disappointment.

      I am at your command.

Half the things you do might just as well be turned over to me.

      For I can do them quickly, correctly and profitably.

I am easily managed; just be firm with me.

      Those who are great, I have made great.

Those who are failures, I have made failures.

      I am not a machine, though I work with the precision of a machine and the intelligence of a person.

You can run me for profit, or you can run me for ruin.

Show me how you want it done. Educate me. Train me.

Lead me. Reward me.

And I will then do it automatically.

I am your servant.

Who am I?

I am a habit.

For the first 20 years of my adult life, I didn't practice some of the essential principles of leadership, but I did have a fair amount of discipline. I spent over 20 years as a recording artist... I recorded seven national albums, performed over 2000 concerts, had been on TV countless times — and accumulated 132 rejection letters before I was finally signed to RCA records at age 37.

I cannot give you the formula for
            success, but I can give you the
formula for failure, which is:
            try to please everybody.

⊞ HERBERT BAYARD SWOPE ⊞

DISCIPLINE, DRIVE & DETERMINATION

Although I had seemingly achieved the American dream, it was full of holes. One of the unfortunate realities of being a recording artist is that you usually end up spending more money than you make in trying to further your career. So when I was dropped from RCA at 40, I was virtually broke. That may seem to be a strange time to attempt to start a multi-million dollar business, but I developed an inner belief that I could find a way and beat the odds. I took my last $2000, hired a bulldozer to clear some land on my farm and began

ROCK SOLID
LEADERSHIP

You *never will* be the person you can be,
if *pressure*, *tension* and *discipline*
are taken out of your life.

▫ HERBERT BAYARD SWOPE ▫

my journey. Every day I woke up with a commitment to do whatever it takes; to barter, to borrow or to work on that studio complex as a carpenter. Three and one half years later I had managed to create several large timber frame buildings which now hold four separate recording studios, as well as kitchens, lounges, media rooms, apartments and offices.

"The important thing is this: to be able at any moment to sacrifice what we are for what we can become."

▣ CHARLES DUBOIS ▣

THE RESULTS

Nine years from the time I first hired that bulldozer, Dark Horse Recording has become one of the most successful studio complexes in the world. Artists like Faith Hill, Neil Diamond, The Judds, Michael W. Smith, Alison Krauss, Michael McDonald, Amy Grant and countless others all come here to record. Thomas Edison once said, "Opportunity is missed by most people because it is dressed in overalls and looks like work." The only way I was ever able to bring this business into existence was to discipline myself to put one foot in front of the other, day in and day out, no matter how excruciating it was to weather constant storms, setbacks and adversities.

Your success in *any* business
will always be in direct proportion to
your ability to consistently *exceed expectations*
of your customers.

◻ **ROBIN CROW** ◻

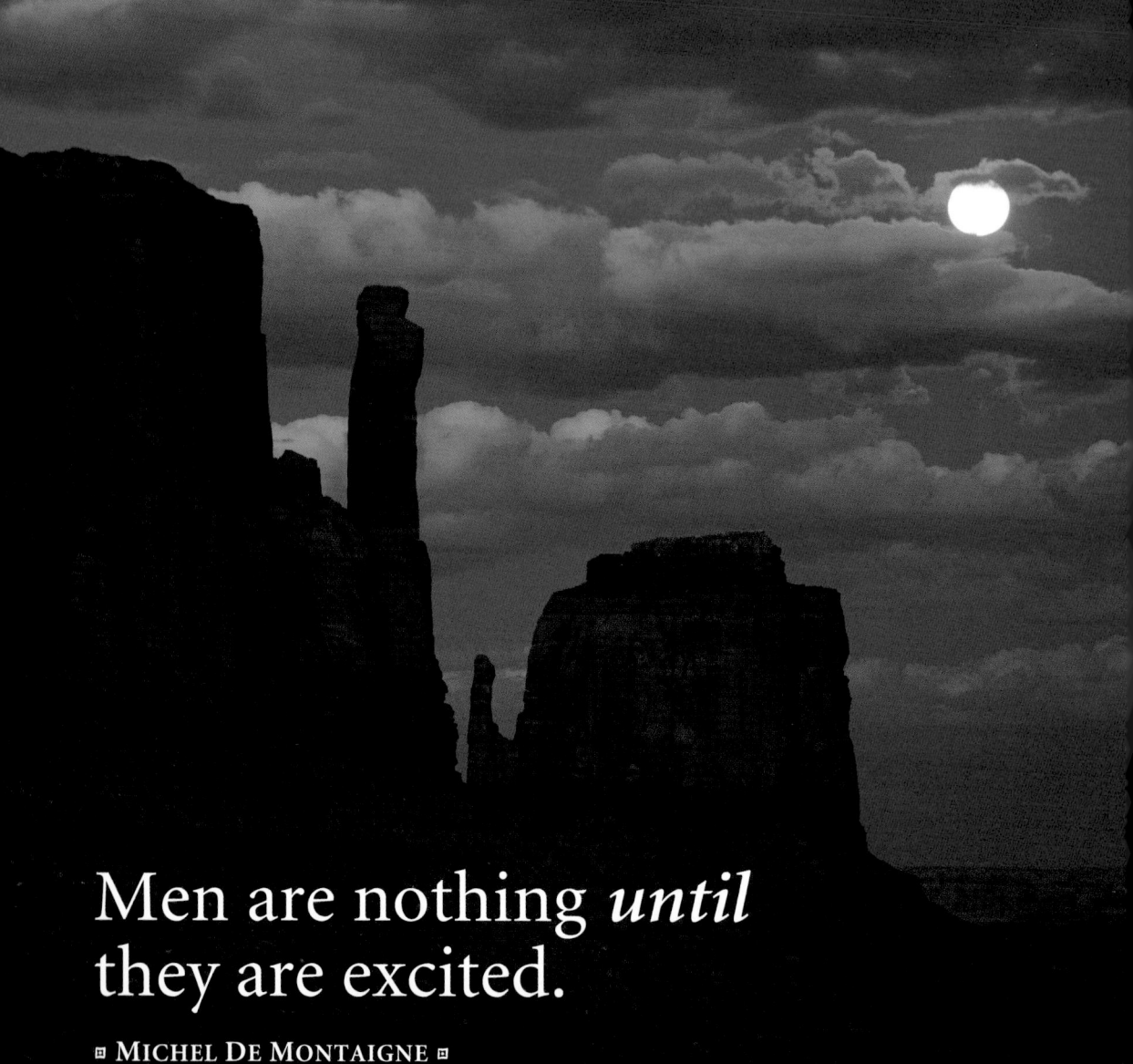

Men are nothing *until* they are excited.

◙ MICHEL DE MONTAIGNE ◙

ENTHUSIASM

As we all know, enthusiasm is another primary key to leadership. Everyone has heard stories about the enthusiasm and spirit of Southwest Airlines, but over the last ten years I've had the opportunity to view that airline from the inside out. My sister, Laura, works at the Dallas corporate headquarters as an Employee Communication Publications Team Leader… which really means she's a writer for the monthly news magazine. Of course

Employee Communication Publications Team Leader does have a good ring to it. For years, Laura has told me stories about Herb Kelleher, the founder and chairman of the board of Southwest. She talked about how his enthusiasm has permeated the company with his eccentric but lovable and very effective style of leadership. Laura's office is just down the hall from Herb's. She says it's not uncommon for him to see her, give her a hug and say, "I simply don't know what this company would do without you." IMAGINE THAT. Nothing could be more motivating. And she pays him back with loyalty beyond compare. She could earn two or three times as much using her journalism skills elsewhere, but she won't even consider it. That kind of loyalty is priceless.

Once, when my travels took me through Dallas, Laura and I went out for a Saturday dinner at a Mexican restaurant just a few miles from the Southwest Airlines corporate headquarters. I asked if I could see where she works. When we entered the building, which is home to over 3000 employees, I noticed over the elevator, etched in glass, was the Southwest Airlines mission statement.

"The mission of Southwest Airlines is dedication to the highest quality of Customer Service delivered with a sense of warmth, friendliness, individual pride and Company Spirit."

Nothing too unusual about that, except for the fact it didn't even mention planes. Then, as I walked off the elevator onto the second floor, I was overwhelmed by these endless hallways which were filled with thousands of pictures. I wish you could have been there. There were photos of employees at charity ballgames, Christmas parties and company picnics. There were letters from celebrities and business competitors. There were articles and clippings about Southwest as well as posters and brochures from the early days when the airline was just getting started.

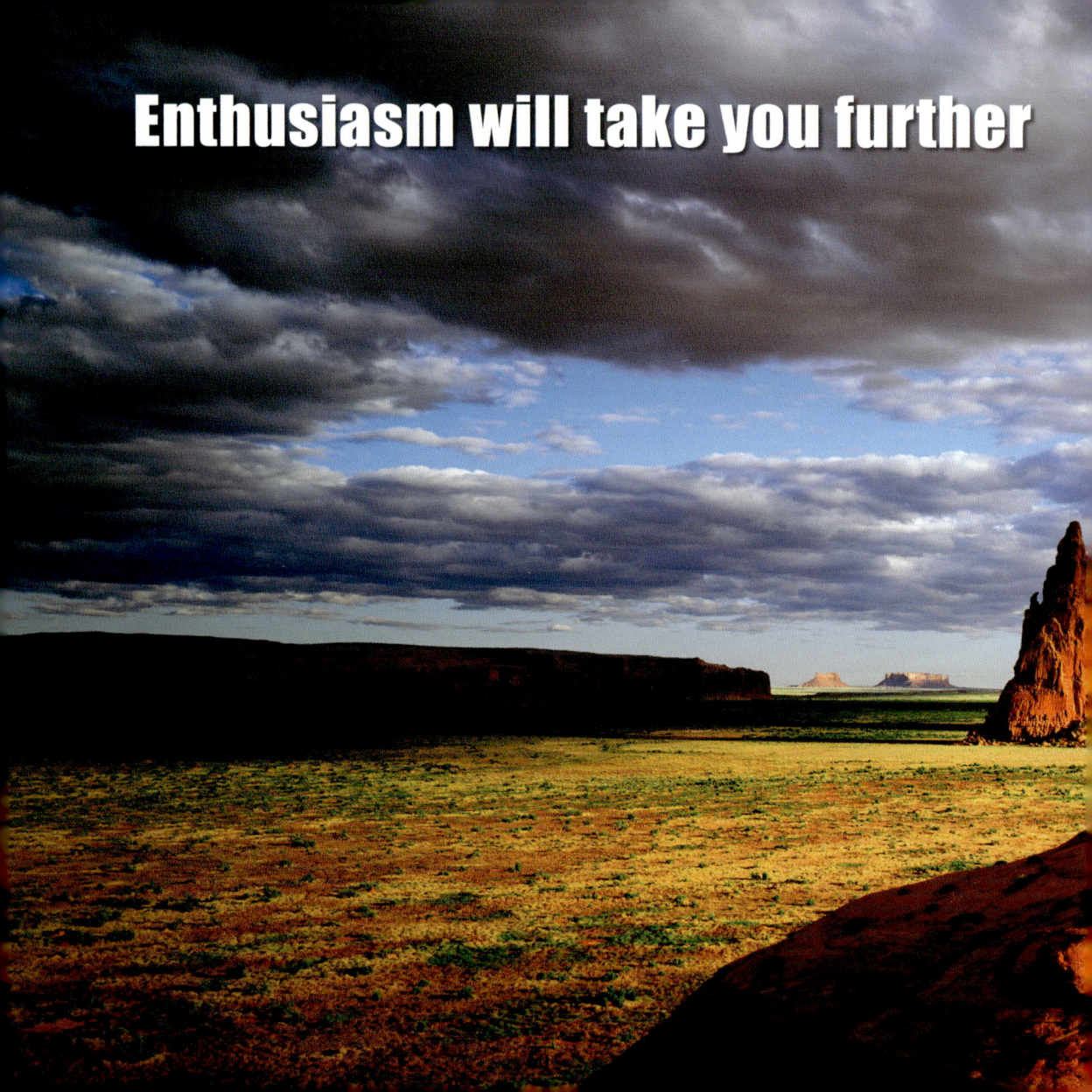

Enthusiasm will take you further

than talent, title or skill. ▫ ROBIN CROW ▫

HERE'S THE STORY

When Southwest Airlines built their headquarters about 15 years ago, they decided to fill their walls with photos and memorabilia. President Colleen Barrett (known as the "heart" of the company) began the tradition of asking employees to submit their own mementos to represent their personal lives and their experiences at Southwest. The result is basically an enormous company scrapbook. I saw a cheerleading uniform, an old flight attendant uniform, and my favorite, a crushed tuba (although it did make me think twice about checking my guitar as luggage) — all matted and framed behind glass. Each picture is a piece of what makes Southwest Airlines one of the most extraordinary companies in the world. These halls went on seemingly forever. Imagine, it's a

If you're *not fired* with enthusiasm,

five-story building and those photos are on every level, floor to ceiling. There was one hallway completely devoted to photos of employees and their pets. It was like the **Smithsonian of employee appreciation**. But as I started looking more closely at the photos, I noticed that most of them included at least one picture with Herb hanging out with that employee at a staff picnic or some other celebration — always laughing and having a great time. It became so obvious to me that Herb's enthusiasm and spirit of celebration is at the core of what Southwest stands for as a company. And let me tell you, at Southwest they know how to celebrate. They know the importance of having fun at work. Laura says that it's not uncommon to see a spontaneous parade marching through headquarters in the

you *will be fired* with enthusiasm.

◦ VINCE LOMBARDI ◦

ENTHUSIASM *is at the bottom of all progress.*
With it there is accomplishment.

Without it there are only excuses. ▫ HENRY FORD ▫

middle of a busy workday, or to see a department playing a game of hackey sack in the hallway or testing out their long jump skills. As all this was sinking in I began to understand why Southwest's mission statement focused in on "Customer Service, individual pride and Company Spirit" over talking about airplanes. Southwest Airlines is all about people serving people.

THE RESULTS

While some of America's mammoth airlines are filing bankruptcy, Southwest is thriving and in the black. In fact, they are now celebrating 33 consecutive years of profitability and their market value is more than the next four airlines combined.

Nothing is more attractive and more motivating than a leader who takes the positive view, especially during times of great adversity. People will come out of the woodwork to participate in an atmosphere of excitement, passion and optimism. Your level of success as a leader will be in direct proportion to your level of enthusiasm.

RELENTLESS OPTIMISM

Look at it this way… make the decision to be enthusiastic… not only will it put you in a positive state… you will have a positive impact on all those around you. Make the decision to be enthusiastic and you'll achieve every goal with greater ease, people will stick with you through thick and thin and most importantly, everyone will have more fun.

Every man is enthusiastic at times. One man
has enthusiasm for *thirty minutes,* another man
has it for *thirty days.* But it is the man who has it for
thirty years who makes a success in life.

▣ EDWARD B. BUTLER ▣

A great leader never sets himself above his followers except in carrying responsibilities.

⊞ JULES ORMONT ⊞

RESPONSIBILITY

Bear Bryant, the legendary Alabama football coach, was once asked what was the key to his coaching success. He thought for a second and said, "When we win I give them (the players) all the credit and when we lose I take all the blame." He smiled and walked away. When things go wrong, great leaders take full responsibility for the results. **No excuses.** Harry Truman made this clear when he uttered his famous four words… **"The buck stops here!"**

In one of Ronald Reagan's cabinet meetings, General Colin Powell presented an idea he was passionate about. This discussion went on for about an hour with Reagan asking tough questions because he felt the proposal had flaws. In the end, however, he said, "Colin, it's your call. If you think it will work, we'll go for it."

A few months later, however, Reagan was grilled at a news conference because the plan had failed miserably. One of the reporters asked the question, "Whose idea was this; yours or someone else's?" Reagan didn't hesitate, he said, "I take full responsibility." He then glanced at Powell sitting in the front row and saw tears welling in his eyes.

After the news conference, Powell walked over to a friend and said, "I'd do anything for that man."

ROCK SOLID
LEADERSHIP

No individual rain
drop ever considers
itself responsible
for the flood.

▪ JOHN RUSKIN ▪

CHARACTER — *the willingness to accept*
is the source from which

74

responsibility for one's own life — self-respect springs. ◘ JOAN DIDION ◘

Let's take a second and look at how taking responsibility applies to my business, Dark Horse Recording.

- *When people under my employ don't come across warm and hospitable on the phone, whose responsibility is it?*

- *If my electric bill skyrockets because one of my employees left all thirteen central air systems on over the Christmas holidays, whose responsibility is it?*

- *If one of my biggest clients starts recording elsewhere… because we weren't up on our game… perhaps a grounding problem… or some of the equipment wasn't working to 100% satisfaction… whose responsibility is it?*

- *If my bills don't get paid… If my invoices don't get collected… If lightning strikes and wipes out Bill's computer files in the front office because they weren't backed up… whose responsibility is it?*

IT'S MINE.

I guess you can see where I'm going with this. Bottom line, these things are all MY RESPONSIBILITY.

Remember, failure to hit the bull's eye is never the fault of the target. That's why successful leaders focus on responsibility over blame.

Many people want to wear the cloak of leadership, but remember, with it comes the burden of responsibility.

It is easy to dodge our responsibilities,
the consequences

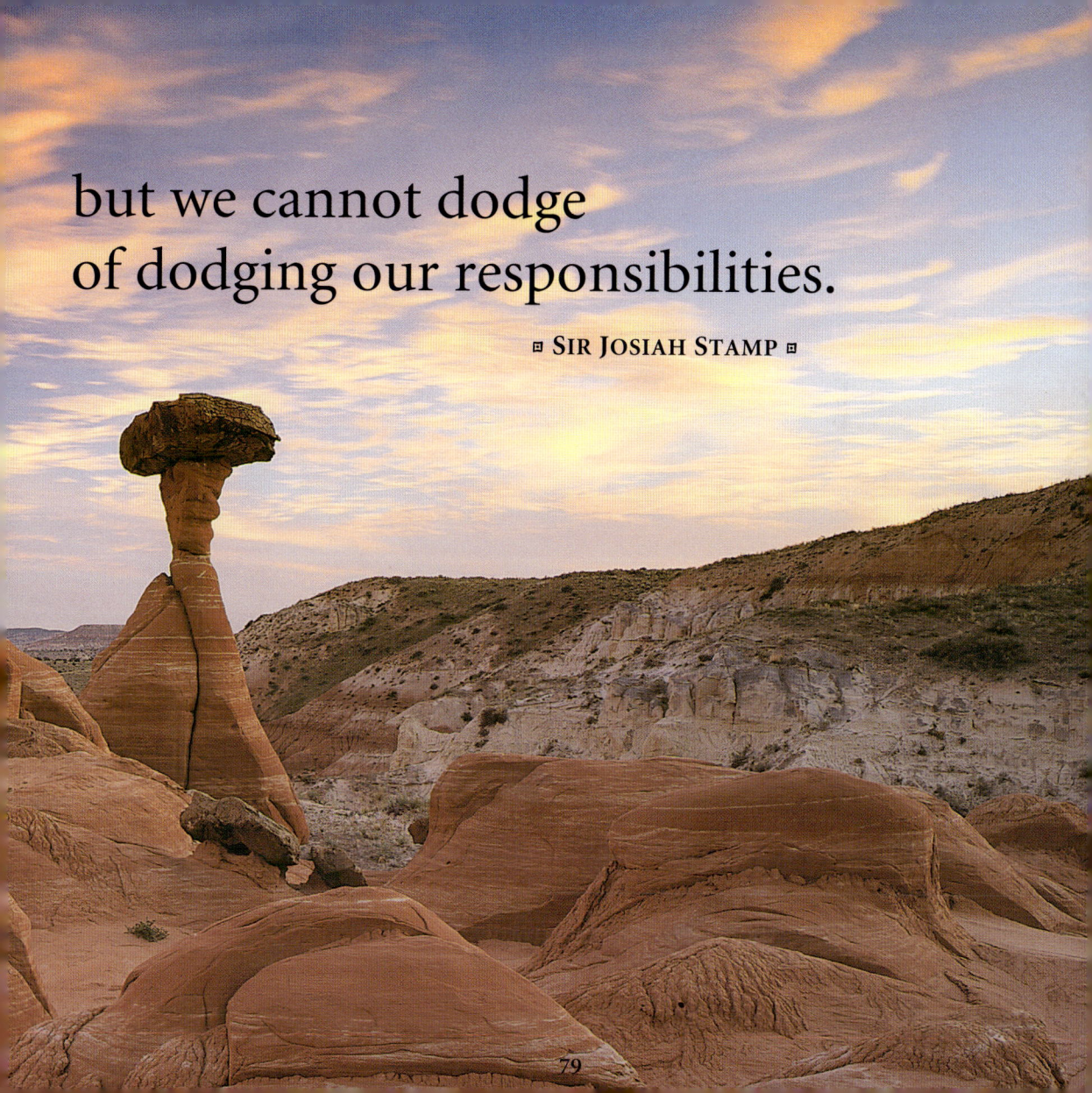

but we cannot dodge
of dodging our responsibilities.

◻ SIR JOSIAH STAMP ◻

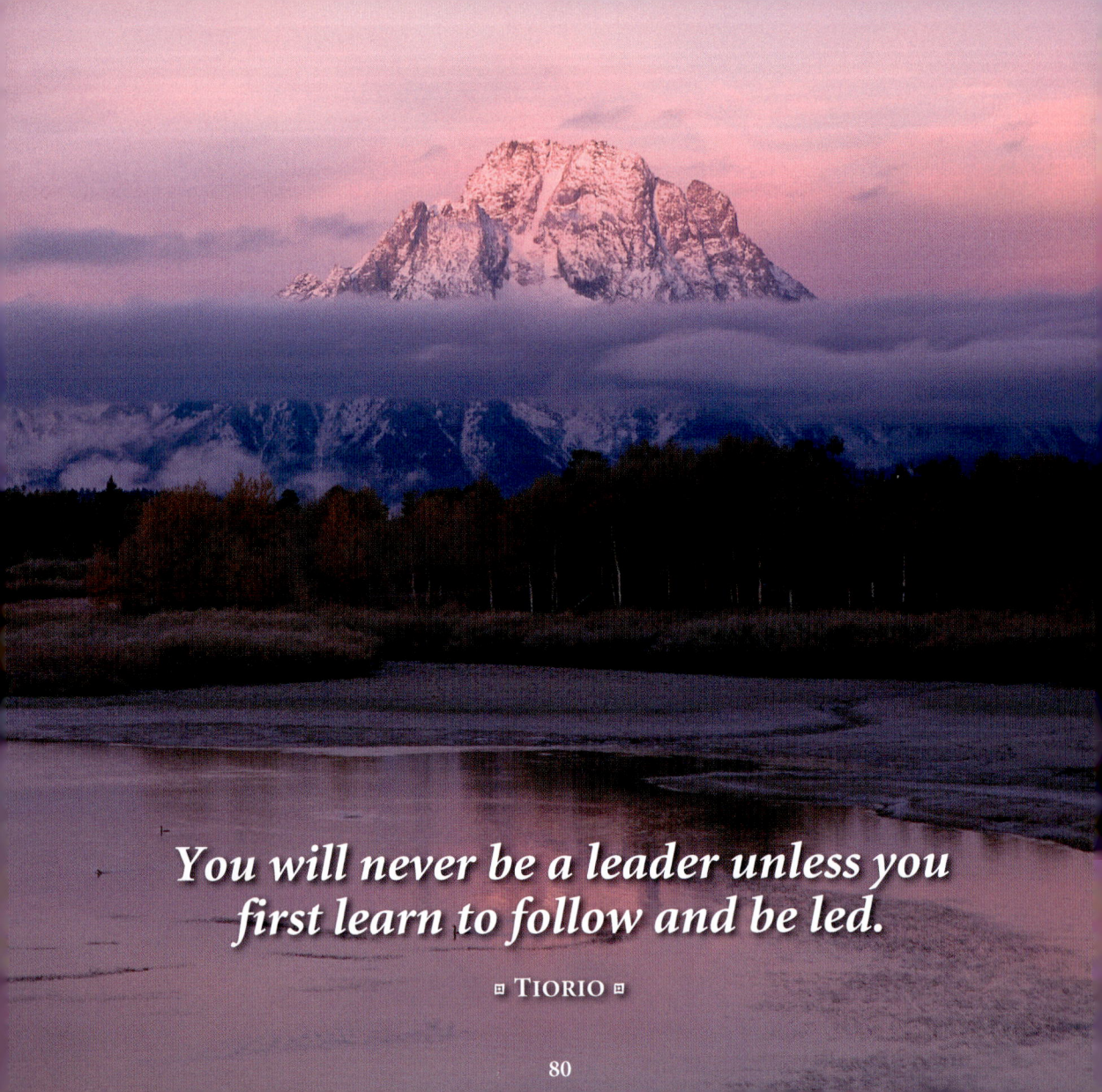

You will never be a leader unless you first learn to follow and be led.

▫ TIORIO ▫

SACRIFICE

Anything worth pursuing comes at a price. Parents will sacrifice creature comforts, they will work overtime or pick up a second job to make sure their children get a good education. Small business owners will work 24/7 or refuse to pay themselves to make sure they can continue to make payroll for their employees. Sometimes the cost is high, but the more you are willing to sacrifice in the short term, the greater the long-term rewards will be.

One of my favorite places to eat is a restaurant called J Alexander's in Nashville. Years ago, I made a mistake ordering and the waitress picked up on it, so she insisted on starting over with another meal. A few minutes later the manager came by, introduced himself, and informed me my meal would be on the house. As you might imagine, this made a big impression on me. Think about it… they sacrificed a twenty dollar invoice in trade for my long-term loyalty. And that's just what they got. I've since eaten there probably a hundred times. Some-

The prime role of a leader
is to *offer an example* of
courage and sacrifice.

◻ REGIS DEBRAY ◻

times when there's a long wait, or something's not quite right,
they'll bring me a free dessert or a complimentary appetizer. They
understand that superior customer service and sacrifice is an
ongoing process. More importantly, sacrifice is the ultimate example
of walking your talk. Remember, sacrifice is not a one-time event;
it's a continual process that leads to a higher level of leadership.

To exceed the expectations of others, we

must first raise expectations of ourselves.

▫ ROBIN CROW ▫

The wise person possesses humility.
He knows that the small island
of knowledge is surrounded by
a vast sea of the unknown.

⊞ HAROLD C. CHASE ⊞

HUMOR AND HUMILITY

When it comes to understanding the power of humor and humility in leadership, Ronald Reagan was the master. He realized that laughter creates a bond between people like nothing else. He also realized that laughter, especially poking fun at yourself, could defuse almost any issue. A great example of this

Humility is the most difficult of all virtues to achieve; nothing dies harder than the desire to think well of one's self.

▪ T.S. ELIOT ▪

is that in his first campaign debate against Walter Mondale, Mr. Mondale raised concerns about Reagan's age (70), when Reagan gave a confused, uninformed performance. However, at the next debate, Reagan defused the issue with humor. He looked right at the audience and said, "I will not make age an issue of this campaign. I am not going to exploit, for political purposes, my opponent's youth and inexperience." The crowd roared with laughter and the age issue was hardly mentioned again in the campaign.

Humility leads to *strength* and *not to weakness.*
It is the highest form of self-respect to *admit*
mistakes and to make amends for them.

▫ JOHN J. MCCLOY ▫

Even after the assassination attempt on his life, he used humor to put the nation at ease. It was reported that when he first saw his wife, Nancy, at the hospital, he looked up with a smile and said, "Honey, I forgot to duck." Also, as the doctors approached the operating table, he looked at one of his Cabinet members who was at his side and said with a smile… "I hope he's a Republican."

We should never forget the power of humor and humility when it comes to effective leadership.

The one important thing I have learned over the years is the difference between taking one's *work* seriously and taking one's *self* seriously. The first is imperative and the second is disastrous.

▣ **MARGOT FONTEYN** ▣

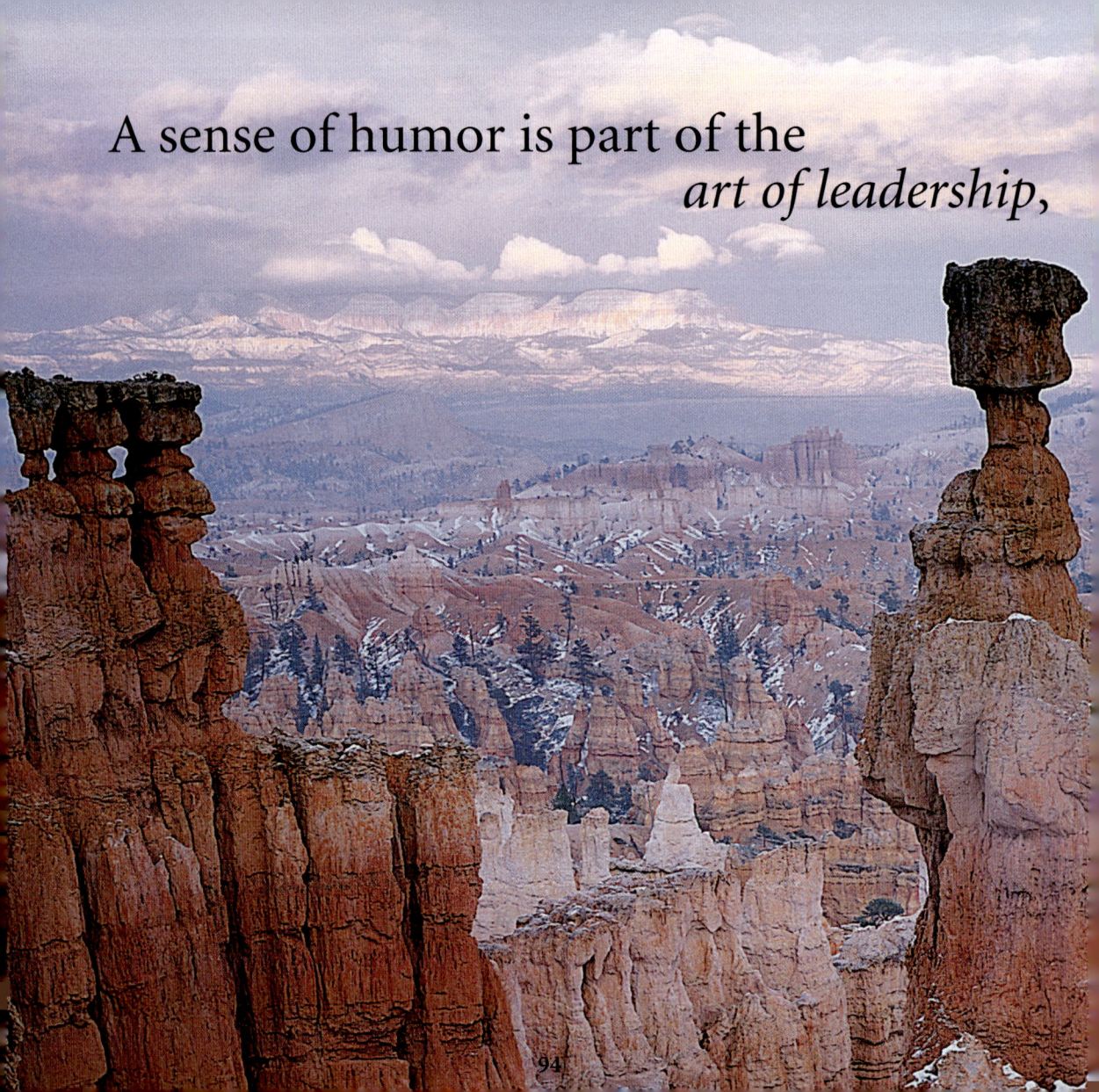

A sense of humor is part of the
art of leadership,

of getting along
    with people, of getting things done.

    ◼ DWIGHT D. EISENHOWER ◼

**Perhaps the most central characteristic
of authentic leadership is the relinquishing of
the impulse to dominate others.**

▫ DAVID COOPER ▫

INFLUENCE

Mary Kay Ash, the founder of Mary Kay Cosmetics, was loved by her people. When she would walk into a room she said she used to pretend there was an invisible sign around everyone's neck that said: "Make me feel important." Recent studies, in fact, have shown that appreciation and recognition can be even more important than wages or working conditions. Dr. Abraham Maslow, a famous psychologist, once said "Recognition

The *crux of leadership* is that you must constantly stop to consider how *your decisions* will *influence* people.

▫ MICHIGAN STATE POLICE MAXIM ▫

is a need that we all crave; there are no exceptions." And one of your greatest challenges as a leader is to fill that need in your people. Well-chosen, well-timed, sincere words of praise and encouragement are key. Leaders can use their influence to achieve extraordinary results from ordinary people, not by lighting a fire beneath them, but by building a fire WITHIN them.

A FEW TIPS...

● **Use the 5 to 1 method.** For every one time you offer constructive criticism, make sure to acknowledge them for five things they've done right.

● **Praise them on the spot.** The sooner you praise them after the event, the more meaningful it is to them. So praise while the moment is hot.

● **Acknowledge them publicly for others to see.** There's nothing more important to people than significance and recognition.

● **Find creative ways to reward good behavior.** Unexpected rewards like giving extra time off or spontaneously taking that person to lunch will reap great dividends.

Take it from me, a veteran performer, there's nothing like the sound of applause.

It's simple… go the extra mile and *you will stand out* from crowd. ROBIN CROW

The very *exercise of leadership*
fosters capacity for it.

⬚ CYRIL FALLS ⬚

102

THE STARS CAN'T SHINE
UNTIL THE SUN GOES DOWN

Get out of your team's way and let them perform. Bold words they are, but actually putting that philosophy into action is not as easy as it sounds. Many leaders — because of fear, a need for control, or sheer insecurity — want to micro-manage everything, which leaves little room for developing new leaders and letting team members shine. ***Who knows what brilliant ideas might be lurking in the minds of your employees?*** Simply asking the question, "What do you think?" can engage people in your organization and give them a sense of ownership and participation. That leads to greater loyalty, higher productivity and the will to achieve excellence. Remember, getting another person to participate is the very essence of leadership. And that's how you'll inspire your staff to exceed expectations.

A determination to succeed is the only way to succeed that I know anything about.

◘ WILLIAM FEATHER ◘

104

PERSEVERANCE

Perseverance is at the root of exceeding expectations. Though there have been many detours, roadblocks and potholes along the way, it's the one word that best describes any success I've achieved in my own life. Every leader in any position will face adversity. It's not a matter of if, but when. How you handle it is critical to your success in business and in life. Trust me, I know how hard it is in the real world. It's hard to stay enthusiastic when you work for weeks without seeing any visible progress. It's difficult to be positive when stacks of unpaid bills are piling up. It's not easy to remain excited in the face of rejection after rejection. It's painful to keep persevering day in and day out when you're running on empty. Why do some people buckle under the pressure while others somehow find the strength to carry on when the going gets rough?

In the realm of *ideas*,
everything depends on
enthusiasm; in the real world,
all rests on *perseverance*.

◘ JOHANN WOLFGANG VON GOETHE ◘

I have three keys to persevering:

1

ONE STEP AT A TIME

This may sound too simple to feel important, but it's an "attitude" we need to embrace. Short term, realistic goals are key. Remember… "Inch by inch life's a cinch; yard by yard life is hard." Each day you should try to close the gap between where you are and where you want to be.

Those who say it *cannot be done*
should *not interrupt* the person doing it.

▫ CHINESE PROVERB ▫

2

BUILD MOMENTUM

Albert Einstein said that compound interest was the most powerful force in our society. Persevering is much like the principle of compound interest — the longer you stay committed and work toward your goals, the more momentum you'll build and the greater the rewards will be. In the beginning, you may see very little progress, but gradually you'll begin stacking one success on top of another, until soon your momentum will make you a force to be reckoned with.

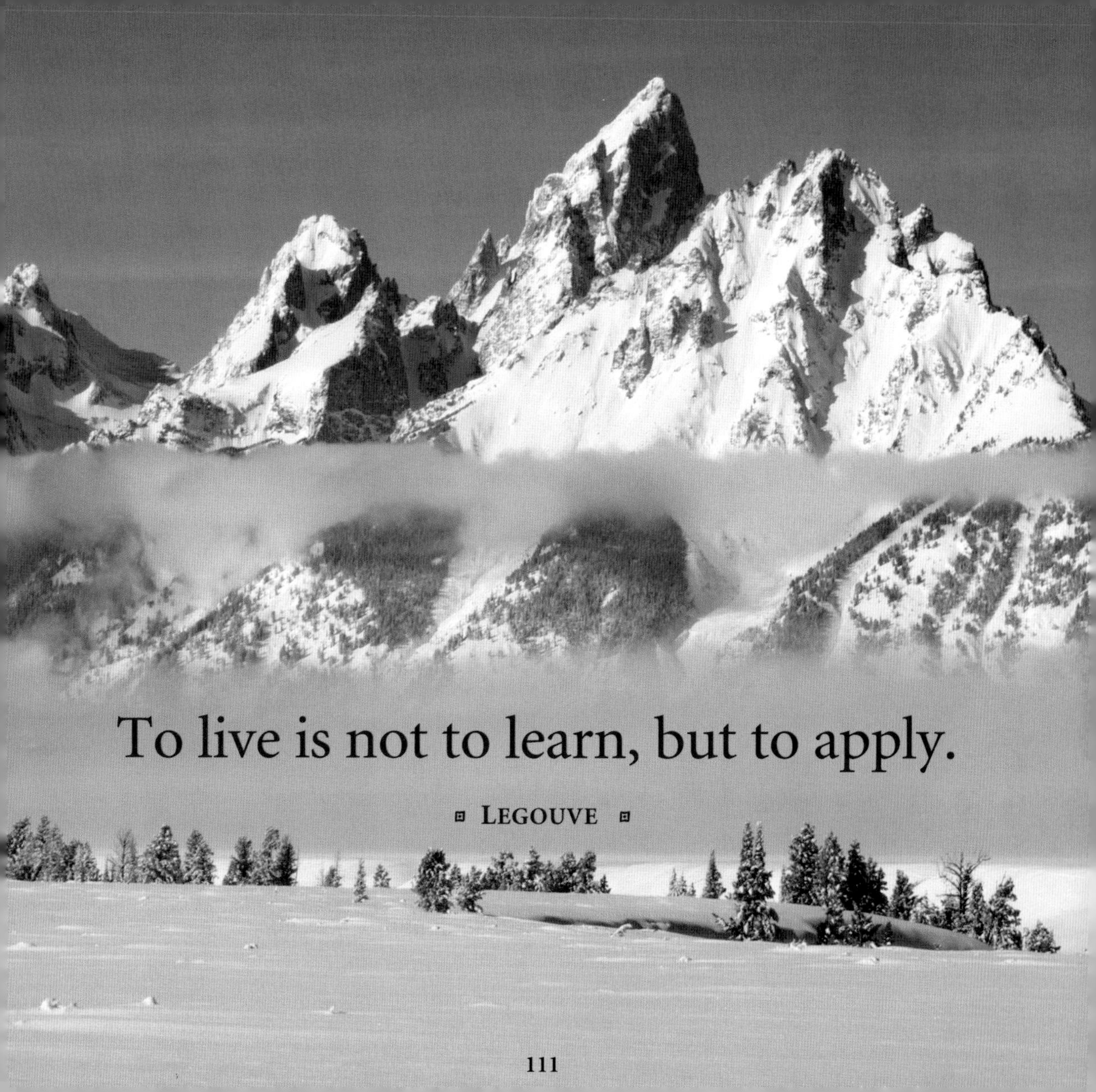

To live is not to learn, but to apply.

⊡ LEGOUVE ⊡

Being willing to do what others will not

will always give you the *competitive edge.*

◻ ROBIN CROW ◻

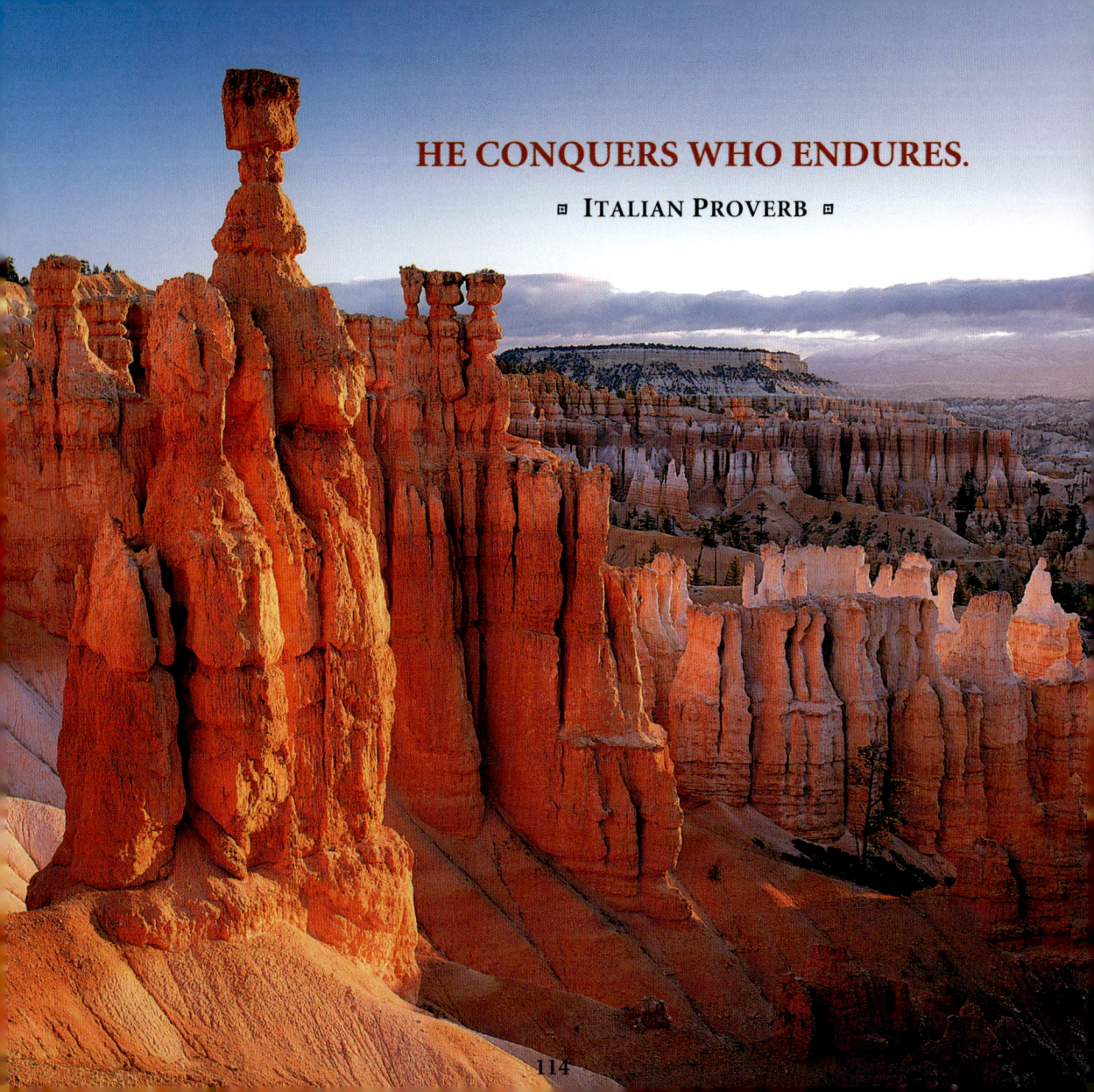

HE CONQUERS WHO ENDURES.

▣ **ITALIAN PROVERB** ▣

3

RESILIENCE

One thing is certain — no matter what your pursuit is, you will experience adversities and setbacks along the way. How you respond to each crisis will determine your level of success. Maybe there's nothing we can do about many events that crash down on us, but it's up to each of us to decide what happens next. The way we interpret and respond to each setback will either make us stronger or weaker. Henry Ford said it best, "Failure is only the opportunity to begin again, more intelligently."

PERSEVERANCE is failing 19 times
and succeeding the 20th.

◘ J. ANDREWS ◘

The next time you're thinking about how hard it is to persevere with your plans, remember, **"Steady on wins the race."** So consider how some of the world's greatest achievements were realized one step at a time, one day at a time, while overcoming one setback at a time. They were accomplished through the power of perseverance. That's when the human spirit triumphs. That's **how great leaders exceed expectations.**

All the *performances*
of human art, at
which we look with
praise or wonder, are
instances of the resistless
force of *perseverance*.

◧ SAMUEL JOHNSON ◧

Robin Crow

Robin has forged a remarkable career on his journey from struggling musician to national recording artist, and then on to his startling success as entrepreneur and business owner. His company, Dark Horse Recording, a four studio complex he built from the ground up, has set the gold standard for customer service and excellence in the recording industry and is home to Faith Hill, Neil Diamond, Michael W. Smith, Jewel and Alison Krauss, to name a few. As a speaker, performer and author, Robin has presented at over 2000 events, has had four books published, released ten albums, appeared on countless television shows and is a featured speaker for Nightingale Conant. Robin lives in Franklin, TN and serves on the boards of several organizations. He loves spending time enjoying some of his greatest passions — hanging out with his four children, throwing large barbecues for his studio clients and friends, and spending as much time as possible in the Rocky Mountains.

For information about Robin Crow visit:

www.robincrow.com
www.darkhorserecording.com

To discover great way to inspire *friends* and *family,*
or to thank your best *customers* and *employees.*

please visit us at:

www.simpletruths.com

Or call us toll free…

800-900-3427

The
simple truths®
DIFFERENCE

If you have enjoyed this book we invite you to check out our entire collection of gift books, with free inspirational movies, at **www.simpletruths.com.**

You'll discover it's a great way to inspire *friends* and *family,* or to thank your best *customers* and *employees.*

There is one thing in life that took me a long time to learn, and that's ... less is almost always more. This "simple truth" is the foundation on which our company was built. I wanted to create beautiful gift books that anyone can read in less than thirty minutes.

To make each book special, we focused on three things:
1. Great content
2. Great graphics
3. Great packaging to create a *"wow effect"*

Satisfied customers are our #1 priority, so I encourage you to give us feedback on how we're doing. If we ever disappoint you, I hope you'll let us know, and we will do everything we can to make it right. Please send your comments to:

Simple Truths Feedback
1935 Brookdale Road, Suite 139
Naperville, IL 60563

or call toll free ... *800-900-3427*